TRAVELLING
WILD

EXPEDITION TO THE ARCTIC

CP/4

WAYLAND
www.waylandbooks.co.uk

Published in paperback in 2014 by Wayland

Copyright © Wayland 2014

Wayland
Hachette Children's Books
338 Euston Road
London NW1 3BR

Wayland Australia
Level 17/207 Kent Street
Sydney NSW 2000

Commissioning Editor: Debbie Foy
Designer: Lisa Peacock
Consultant: Michael Scott
Proofreader/indexer: Susie Brooks
Map illustrator: Tim Hutchinson

A catalogue for this title is available from
the British Library
910.9'113

ISBN: 978 0 7502 8324 3

Printed in China

10 9 8 7 6 5 4 3 2 1

Wayland is a division of Hachette Children's Books,
an Hachette UK Company.

www.hachette.co.uk

CONTENTS

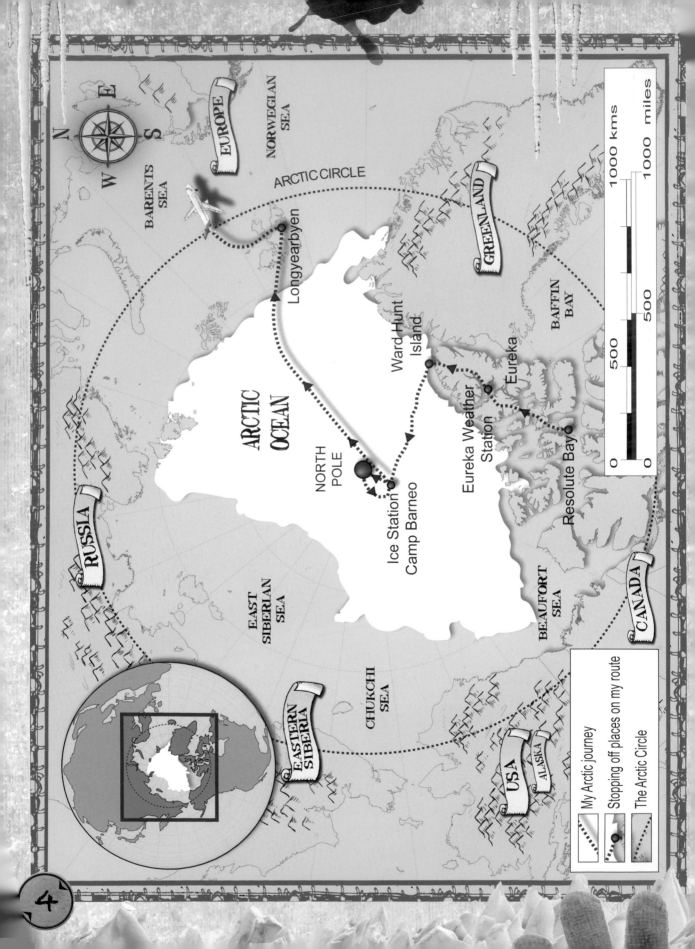

EUROPE

NORWEGIAN SEA

ARCTIC CIRCLE

GREENLAND

BARENTS SEA

BAFFIN BAY

N
W — E
S

Longyearbyen

Ward Hunt Island

Eureka

ARCTIC OCEAN

Eureka Weather Station

NORTH POLE

Resolute Bay

Ice Station Camp Barneo

RUSSIA

CANADA

EAST SIBERIAN SEA

BEAUFORT SEA

CHUKCHI SEA

EASTERN SIBERIA

USA

ALASKA

1000 kms

1000 miles

500

500

0

0

My Arctic journey

Stopping off places on my route

The Arctic Circle

4

JOURNEY TO THE NORTH POLE

Preparing for the trip

I'm finally on my way! Tomorrow, I will be travelling with my team to Resolute Bay in Canada, ready to embark on our 55—day expedition to the North Pole. I've spent months training for this, including winter nights in the hills near my home, pulling heavy tyres attached to my body harness to get used to hauling the sledge across the frozen Arctic wastes. Now I can't wait to get going!

Land of the midnight sun

The Arctic is the northernmost part of the Earth. It is basically a vast, ice—covered ocean, surrounded by permanently frozen land called permafrost. In the Arctic during summer, the sun is visible for 24 hours a day, but during winter it doesn't appear at all. For explorers, an expedition to the North Pole — the Earth's most northerly point — is the ultimate challenge. The extreme cold, treacherous ice and frequent blizzards make this one of the most hostile places on the planet.

Timing

We've planned our trip to last from mid—February until mid—April. By the time May arrives, the ice starts melting and walking becomes hazardous. This means that the first part of our trip will be in darkness, as the sun won't rise until early March, and then will be out for only for half an hour each day at first.

What am I taking?
- sledge and skis
- Gore-Tex® boots, outerwear and balaclava
- polypropylene underwear
- waterproof suit for swimming
- down-lined sleeping bag
- knife
- first-aid kit
- waterproof matches
- torch with extra batteries
- small shovel
- binoculars
- high-protein food bars
- signalling mirror
- zippered plastic bags
- map and compass
- GPS navigation device
- shotgun (for protection from polar bears!)

Days 1–4, 14–17 February

Our plane touched down at Resolute Bay four days ago. It feels very remote here as it's dark and bitterly cold. The Inuit (indigenous people of the Arctic) call this place Qausuittuq, meaning 'place with no dawn', which describes it well! For the first time, I understood what −30 °C with a gale blowing feels like. Already we're learning to look out for the first signs of frostnip and what to do about it. We've settled into our hotel and are busying ourselves with our routines such as collecting food, checking our tents and equipment and acclimatising.

Resolute Bay

Founded in 1947 as a military and scientific base, Resolute Bay now serves as a starting point for Arctic expeditions and has a population of over 200. It boasts a retail store, an airport gift shop, four hotels, a restaurant, a school and a gym, as well as cable TV and the internet. There are very few cars here, and no buses, trains or taxis. Most people get around by snowmobile or on foot. Resolute Bay is the starting point for the Polar Race and the Polar Challenge, in which teams race the 648 km to the North Magnetic Pole (see page 26).

Be smart, survive!

Cold is an even bigger threat to survival than you may think. It decreases your ability to think and weakens your capacity to do anything except to get warm. Cold numbs the mind as well as the body, and saps the will to survive. Therefore, before you venture into the Arctic, it's really important to acclimatise your body to the cold and get used to thinking and operating in that environment.

Climate

Resolute Bay is one of Canada's most northerly settlements and among the coldest inhabited places on Earth, with an average yearly temperature of −16.4 °C. The lowest temperature recorded here is −52.2 °C, and the highest is 18.4 °C. It's very dry here, with just 150 mm of precipitation per year, most of it falling as snow in August and September.

Caribou, or reindeer, are found in the Arctic, from Canada to Russia. They migrate south in the winter, travelling over 2,500 km each year!

Psychological preparation

As well as being physically fit, you have to be mentally strong to succeed as an Arctic explorer. So:

- Have a positive attitude – this will boost your morale and help you think creatively.
- Anticipate fears – build confidence in your ability to function despite them!

GET OUT ALIVE !!

THE INUIT PEOPLE

Day 5, 18 February

Last night we left the comfort of our hotel and spent a night in our tents on the ice, as a rehearsal for the tough times to come. Erecting and dismantling tents in the freezing cold was a lot harder than we imagined! This is our last day in Resolute Bay. A couple of us went into the village to collect fuel for our stoves. While we were there, we got chatting with some of the Inuit locals. They gave us some seal-hunting tips. They also told us a little about their history.

The Inuit diet includes seal, caribou and fish, eaten with roots, berries and seaweed.

Hunters

The Inuit live in the Arctic regions of Greenland, Canada, US and eastern Siberia. Traditionally, they hunted whales, walrus, caribou and seal. They used to use sealskin boats called kayaks (although today motorboats are more common), and in the winter they hunt on the ice using dog sleds (qamutik). As well as eating animal flesh for food, Inuits use their hides, sinews, bones and blubber to make clothing, blankets, cooking oil and bone tools. During the winter, many Inuit build shelters from snow. In the warmer months, some live in tents of animal skins on a frame of bones.

Relocated

In 1953, the Canadian government forced Inuit people from northern Quebec to move to the newly established settlement at Resolute Bay to help introduce Canadian control of the area. The Inuit were promised homes and animals to hunt, but the resettled people found no buildings or familiar animals to hunt. Eventually, they learned to hunt beluga whales and were able to build a life in the area. In 2008, the government paid compensation to the families of the relocated Inuit and issued a formal apology.

Be smart, survive!

To hunt a seal, do as the Inuit do: find a basking one and stay downwind of it, slowly moving closer. If it moves, lie down flat on the ice, raising your head up and down and wriggling your body slightly, imitating the seal's movements. Approach the seal with your body sideways to it and your arms close to your body. When you are within 30 m of the seal, aim your harpoon.

REACHING THE PACK ICE

Days 6-10, 19-23 February

This morning we left Resolute Bay and flew north to Eureka Weather Station (see map on page 4), a remote base where you can hear Arctic wolves howling in the hills above the airstrip. After refuelling, we flew 480 km further north to Ward Hunt Island, on the bleak, frozen edge of the Arctic Ocean. This was the starting point for our trek. It's even colder here than Resolute Bay, and completely dark – the sun won't rise for another three weeks and there's only an hour or two of dim twilight each day. We'll be travelling by moonlight and helmet torch.

Starting the trek

Our first task is to get our bearings. We can't use the North Star, as it's almost directly overhead, so we use our compasses to check which way is north. Permanently attached to the coast of Ward Hunt Island is a wide sheet of ice called an ice shelf. We make good progress across this ice shelf, hauling our sledges across the soft, deep snow and reaching its edge in seven hours. Here we erect our tents, cook and eat a meal and bed down for a few hours.

Polar bear liver

Whatever happens, don't eat the liver of a polar bear as it contains toxic amounts of vitamin A. If you do eat it, symptoms can include drowsiness, severe headache, blurred vision, vomiting and – in some extreme cases – all your skin may peel off!

Ice floes

The Arctic Ocean is covered in giant sheets of ice called ice floes. Collectively the floes are called pack ice. The wind blows the floes south and they shatter against the ice shelf that surrounds Canada's northern coast. Looking out across the frozen ocean, we can see the cracks in the floes, and giant slabs of broken ice heaped on top of each other, forming a 12–metre–high barricade running east to west for several kilometres. To progress, we must first scale this barricade.

A COLD, DARK WORLD

Days 11-15, 24-28 February

Using a rope and pulley system we began hauling ourselves and our sledges over the barricade of ice slabs. It was tiring and dangerous. Between each slab were deep cracks covered with soft snow. We often fell into these, sinking up to our waists. The rubble of shattered ice floes continued for more than a kilometre, making progress slow.

Skiing blind

One of the biggest hazards for a polar explorer in the winter months is the darkness. It's not so bad when the moon is out, but when it slips behind the hills or the clouds, it becomes very hard to make out the details of the scene ahead, despite our helmet torches. We're constantly worried about wandering onto thin ice or falling into a crevasse, which is a deep, open crack in the ice.

Low temperatures

The other danger is the extreme cold at this time of year – at times it can drop as low as –60 °C. At that temperature, simple activities like lighting a cooking stove or erecting a tent can be very difficult and time-consuming. Even going to the toilet can mean risking hypothermia (see pages 16). One of our party lost his sledge beneath an ice slab. When he tried to drag it out of the water, he got deep frostbite in several fingers. As a result, he had to be escorted back to Ward Hunt Island and taken to hospital from there. The fingers will probably have to be amputated.

Be smart, survive!

Fire is important to Arctic explorers. We need it for warmth, cooking and to melt snow or ice for water. There are no trees in the Arctic so we must bring our own fuel. We use a hobo stove to cook on, which is a tin can filled with oil, alcohol, kerosene, wax, even animal dung. For warmth, a single candle can provide enough heat for a one-person tent.

People who live or hunt in the Arctic Circle must get used to long, dark winters when the sun never rises.

How to cross a snow bridge

GET OUT ALIVE!!

Among the hazards we face regularly are snow bridges. These are drifts of snow that form over a crevasse. They look solid, but are extremely thin and fragile. If the snow begins to crack beneath you, then you are probably on a snow bridge. First find the strongest part by poking ahead of you with a pole. Distribute your weight evenly by lying flat and crawling.

TRAVELLING ON THE ICE

Days 16-20, 1-5 March

We're averaging about 20 km a day. We make the best time when there's little ice rubble, and we can put on our skis. One problem has been a lack of snowfall, forcing us to melt sea ice for drinking water, which has a high salt content. It also means we have to use ice screws to pitch our tents – a slow, painstaking process. As I drift off to sleep in my tent, I can hear the ice groaning as it moves beneath us – a strange, unsettling sound.

Negative drift

One of the problems of travelling on ice that floats on an ocean is that it's constantly moving. In our case, the wind is blowing the ice south–east, while we are trying to head north. This is called negative drift. It means we're chasing the Pole, and it's going to add to the length of our journey. The ice is drifting south–east at an average of 0.5 km per hour, so we lose about 2 km every time we go to bed. And although we walk 20 km each day, we only actually achieve 17.5 km.

Be smart, survive!

If the worst happens and you lose your tent in a crevasse or an open water lead (see pages 24-25), you can survive by building yourself a snow cave. First find a snowdrift about 3 m deep, and dig down into it. Keep the roof arched for strength. Build the sleeping platform higher than the entrance and dig a trench between platform and wall to avoid getting wet from melting snow. Walls and ceiling should be at least 30 cm thick. Snow is a great insulator and will keep you warm.

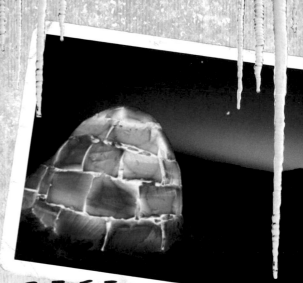

Snow is an excellent insulator, so igloos are surprisingly warm inside.

Pressure ridges

The ice floes that cover the Arctic Ocean are constantly moving because of pressure exerted on them by wind, tides and ocean currents. These forces sometimes cause ice floes to collide, forming great mounds of ice called pressure ridges — mountainous obstacles that we're forced to climb or go around. The above-water part of a pressure ridge is called the sail, and the below-water part is called the keel. Keels can be up to 50 m deep, though most are 10−25 m deep. The height of the sail tends to be about a quarter of the keel's depth.

Days 21-25, 6-10 March

Lars is one of the toughest men in our party, a veteran of several Arctic expeditions, so we were all surprised when he got ill. We noticed him shivering and struggling to eat. He complained of back pain and bleeding when he went to the toilet. Pus came out from under his nails when he squeezed his thumbs. He'd clearly picked up an infection from his various injuries and frostbites. He's refused to give up, though. He's taking antibiotics and struggling on.

A cup of hot tea, sweetened with honey or dextrose, is great for treating hypothermia.

Hypothermia

One of the most serious health risks facing any Arctic explorer is hypothermia. This occurs when the body's temperature falls faster than it can produce heat. The symptoms are uncontrollable shivering, sluggish thinking, and a false feeling of warmth. Severe cases can cause muscle rigidity, unconsciousness, even death. Victims of hypothermia should be made warm by placing them in a sleeping bag and giving them hot, sweet fluids. But care must be taken because warming them up too rapidly can lead to heart failure.

Frostbite

When your skin and other tissues are damaged due to freezing, this is called frostbite. Light frostbite, or frostnip, affects only the skin. Deep frostbite extends below the skin. At very low temperatures, blood vessels near the skin close up, as blood is moved towards the core of the body. This can reduce blood flow to dangerously low levels, leading to the death of tissues. Feet, hands and exposed facial areas are most vulnerable to frostbite. The first sign is loss of feeling. The best way to avoid frostbite is to regularly move your fingers, toes and face muscles.

Be smart, survive!

To prevent frostbite, use the buddy system. Check your friend's face regularly and make sure your friend checks yours. If you get light frostbite, you can rewarm this using heat from other parts of your body or from a companion. Do not attempt to thaw out deep frostbite injuries - this can cause more damage.

Arctic butterfly

Avoid trenchfoot

Trenchfoot happens when your feet are exposed to wet conditions for long periods at a temperature just above freezing. The symptoms are pins and needles, tingling, numbness and pain. The skin will first appear soggy, white and shrivelled, then red, and finally blue or black. The best way to avoid trenchfoot is to keep your feet dry. Carry spare socks in a waterproof bag. Dry your wet socks against your back as you walk.

LIGHT EFFECTS

Days 26-30, 11-15 March

The sun has started to rise for short periods above the horizon. At first, all we could see was a lightening of the sky and the landscape. This was a wonderfully cheering sight, and it meant that we wouldn't be needing our helmet lamps any more. As the sun began to appear, I started spotting strange things in the sky, like halos and upside-down icebergs, and I began to wonder if I was going mad. Erica, a scientist on our team, said it was all due to bent light, ice crystals and atoms colliding.

Aurora Borealis

The most famous light effect of the Arctic is the Aurora Borealis, or Northern Lights. It can look like ribbons or rippling curtains of light, or searchlights across the sky. The colours can be spectacular, ranging from spooky green to neon pink, blue and red. The Aurora Borealis is caused by the solar wind, which is made up of a stream of electrically charged atoms from the sun, colliding with the Earth's atmosphere. The colours vary depending on the type of atom.

Halos

Sometimes you can see rings of light or colour surrounding the sun or the moon. These are caused by light being bent as it shines through clouds of ice crystals. One type of halo, called a 'sun dog', looks like a pair of luminous spots, appearing on either side of the sun. You may also see 'diamond dust' – tiny ice crystals that float in the air and sparkle like diamonds. The bending of light occasionally causes a 'super mirage', when you see an upside-down image of an object above the actual object.

Be smart, survive!

The reflection of the sun's rays off the snow can be so bright it can cause snow blindness. Your eyes get red, teary and painful as if a piece of grit is stuck in them. To treat snow blindness, bandage your eyes until they feel better. You can prevent snow blindness by wearing wrap-around sunglasses. Smearing soot under your eyes will also reduce glare.

POLAR WILDLIFE

Days 31–35, 16–20 March

Two nights ago, I heard a snuffling sound outside my tent. This was followed by a ripping noise. I looked up and saw the head of a polar bear right above me. I screamed. The animal was probably as shocked as me, and it quickly backed away. It ran off with some food. This morning, we found evidence of another polar bear visit. Our rubber boat had been dragged 100 m away and was all chewed up. It took us hours to repair it.

Polar bears

These fierce predators of the Arctic are specially adapted to the icy conditions, with a thick layer of body fat and a water–repellent coat. They eat mainly ringed and bearded seals. They hunt by waiting by a seal's breathing hole. When the bear smells the seal's breath, it reaches into the hole and drags it onto the ice, then kills it by crushing its skull in its jaws. Some studies suggest that polar bear attacks on humans are becoming more frequent due to global warming (see pages 24–25).

Whales

There are 17 species of cetaceans (whales, dolphins and porpoises) in the Arctic. Some, like the narwhal and beluga, stay here all year round. Others, such as the humpback and gray whales, migrate to the Arctic during the summer months to give birth. We were lucky enough to see a pod of belugas (see right). They're white with bulbous heads, and they make loud chirps and clicks, which have earned them the nickname 'the canaries of the sea'. They seemed intrigued by us, and swam close to the edge of our ice floe for several hundred metres.

Birds

Because the Arctic winters are so harsh, very few birds stay there during the colder months. Those that do include certain types of ptarmigan and guillemot, the gyrfalcon, redpoll, snowy owl and little auk. Ptarmigans and redpolls dive into snow banks and use the snow to insulate themselves from the coldest weather. Snowy owls grow feathers on their legs to help keep themselves warm through the winter.

Snowy owl

Avoid getting attacked by a polar bear

GET OUT ALIVE !!

- In most areas with polar bears, you're not allowed to travel unless one of your party is licensed to use a shotgun. Shoot only as a very last resort!
- Don't act like prey – stand your ground. If you run away, the bears are more likely to see you as a meal. Plus, they're faster than you.
- If a bear approaches, act like a threat, stand tall and act aggressively.
- Use bear spray (a form of pepper spray that irritates bears' eyes).

HUMAN HABITATION

Days 36-40, 21-25 March

We have reached Camp Barneo. After so many weeks of seeing nothing ahead of us but ice and more ice, it was amazing to see flags fluttering on the horizon and a plane on the landing strip. We were given a warm welcome by the Russian staff, and were so relieved to be shown to our heated tents with comfortable bedding. There was a doctor to tend to our injuries, and we were even treated to a concert on our first evening.

Annual ice camp

Because of the shifting ice, no permanent base can be established on the Arctic Ocean. Instead, each year, the Russian Geographical Society establishes a temporary base near the North Pole. Camp Barneo is built from scratch in late March, then dismantled in late April when the ice begins to melt. Engineers and specialist advisers are dropped by parachute onto the ice, and they set to work building a runway. Once the runway is complete, cargo planes deliver the camp infrastructure. This annual ice camp has been operating since 2002. Sometimes, problems arise which can include fierce winds, blizzards and fog.

Camp Barneo is a temporary ice base near the North Pole, which exists for one month per year.

Facilities

Camp Barneo has heated 12-person tents, a sauna and a large mess tent serving hot meals and 24-hour tea, coffee and snacks. There are specialists on hand, including mechanics, engineers, pilots and a doctor. Regular flights to and from Longyearbyen, Norway, ferry tourists and scientists wishing to visit the North Pole. As well as serving as a base for skiers, Barneo also accommodates divers who are venturing under the polar ice and skydivers jumping over the North Pole. Barneo staff display their musical and artistic skills with ice carving, photo exhibitions and concerts. In 2012, Barneo even hosted a wedding!

Be smart, survive!

Drinking water in the Arctic can be obtained by melting freshwater ice and snow. Remember: trying to melt snow or ice in your mouth takes away vital body heat and may cause internal cold injuries. If you haven't got another heat source, you can use body heat to melt snow by filling a plastic bag with snow and placing the bag between layers of clothing. If you have the choice, melt ice rather than snow, as it takes less time to melt and yields more water.

GLOBAL WARMING

Days 41–45, 26–30 March

It's spring, the temperature's rising, and the ice continues to break up around us. It's started to resemble a mosaic of islands, separated by open water leads, which are channels of water between ice floes. When we come to a lead, we either jump it or we swim across it in a waterproof suit. This big one-piece suit fits over your clothing and boots and traps air so you float. If the lead's really wide, we paddle to the next floe in our rubber dinghy. That's all we're doing these days – walking, swimming and paddling north.

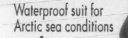

Waterproof suit for Arctic sea conditions

Open water leads

These cracks in the sea ice are caused by a combination of warmer temperatures and ocean currents, and can vary from a few centimetres to a kilometre wide. They may slow our progress, but they're important navigation routes for Arctic mammals and birds. Leads can open and close in just a few hours and shouldn't be confused with polynias – enormous stretches of open water, sometimes hundreds of kilometres wide – which appear in the same place every year. Polynias teem with animal and plant life, as they're the only places where the sun directly reaches the ocean.

Melting ice

The past few decades have witnessed a significant rise in the number
and size of leads, due to global warming. This is the gradual increase
in the temperature of the Earth's atmosphere, partly caused by higher
levels of carbon dioxide from the burning of fossil fuels. Because of
global warming, Arctic sea ice has declined dramatically since 1980 and
massive ice shelves are melting and breaking away. Many Arctic animals
from plankton to polar bears, rely on the sea ice for survival and its
decline threatens their existence.

Melting permafrost

Large parts of the Arctic are made up of permanently frozen ground called
permafrost. As global temperatures increase, the permafrost thaws, causing all
sorts of problems. Roads and buildings constructed on the permafrost may collapse
and pipelines can burst. So-called 'drunken forests', full of fallen trees, have
become another common feature of the warming permafrost. Carbon and methane,
locked in the permafrost for millions of years, may be released as the ground thaws.
These are 'greenhouse gases' and will add to global warming.

REACHING THE POLE

Days 46–50, 31 March–4 April

At last we've arrived! But only just. The last leg of the journey was brutal. First we had these fierce winds against us, slowing us down. Then there was a cold snap, and temperatures plummeted to -60 °C. We drove ourselves onwards through near whiteout conditions. Our faces became so encased in ice, it was hard to find our mouths to put food in, and we couldn't take our mitts off to eat without freezing our fingers. It was looking pretty bleak for a while, but finally we made it! I just can't believe we've reached the North Pole!

On the final part of the journey, conditions were terrible, but sheer willpower saw us through.

Different North Poles

What exactly is the North Pole? It's the northernmost point of the Earth, where the planet's axis of rotation (the point around which it turns) meets its surface. It's sometimes called Geographic North Pole and should not be confused with the North Magnetic Pole, which is where our compasses point to and which constantly moves about due to changes in the Earth's magnetic field.

What did we find there?

When we reached the Geographic North Pole, of course there was nothing to mark it. Unlike the South Pole, the North Pole is located in the middle of an ocean covered with constantly shifting sea ice, so it's impossible to build anything permanent there. What we saw was a flat, featureless plain of ice. The only way we knew we'd arrived was because our GPS read 90° north. Lars, now recovered from his illness, planted a flag. We were quiet for a moment. I admit I shed a tear or two. Then we got to work pitching our tents.

These days, the North Pole has become a popular destination for tourists who come in by helicopter.

Be smart, survive!

Washing yourself in sub-zero temperatures can be pretty uncomfortable, not to say dangerous. One thing I have managed to do from time to time, though, is take a 'snow bath'. Basically, this means taking a handful of snow and washing the areas where sweat accumulates, like under the arms, feet and between the legs.

Whiteout danger

If possible, avoid travelling during a whiteout. This is when visibility is so poor that the horizon completely disappears and there are no reference points to guide you. Whiteouts can be caused by low cloud, mist, fog or blizzards. In these conditions, you might easily get lost or fall through thin ice, a snow bridge or a crevasse. It's far safer to sit tight and wait for better weather.

GET OUT ALIVE!!

27

THE RETURN JOURNEY

Colourful houses at Longyearbyen, Norway

Days 51-55, 5-9 April

The following morning, a helicopter picked us up and flew us back to Camp Barneo. We spent a few more days there before boarding an Antonov AN-74 transport plane to Longyearbyen, Norway. Now I'm back home, I find it hard to describe my emotions. I felt close to death so many times out there in the frozen wasteland, and yet in another way I don't think I've ever felt so alive. It's strange. It's going to be very hard readjusting to normal life.

The future of the Arctic

The stark beauty of the Arctic landscapes is imprinted on my mind — but I worry for its future. Because of global warming (at least partly caused by the fossil fuels humans are burning) scientists are predicting that by 2030 the Arctic Ocean will be entirely ice-free in the summer. Already by 2012, icebreakers and cruise ships were able to sail to the North Pole in late summer. This would affect not just the species living there, but all of us. The melting ice will cause sea levels to rise, resulting in flooding. As the sea ice melts, oil companies will probably move in and start drilling, leading to the possibility of oil spills.

28

Protecting species

Animals such as the caribou, polar bear, walrus and narwhal are facing severe habitat loss due to oil and gas development and Arctic shipping. The conservation group World Wildlife Fund for Nature (WWF) has created maps showing which regions are the most important for these creatures. These can help industries to avoid habitat areas. For example, shipping routes can be altered and pipelines diverted. The WWF is also providing local people with tools and training to enable them to avoid conflict with polar bears.

Ecotourism

Since the 1990s there has been a big rise in the number of tourists visiting the Arctic. Tourism can be a positive force, so long as visitors act responsibly, do not litter, minimise their consumption of natural resources and respect local cultures. Ecotourism, as it is known, allows visitors to appreciate the beauty of the Arctic while at the same time providing income for conservation efforts.

What can we do to help?

One of the first things I did when I got home was to sign Greenpeace's 'Flag for the Future' scroll, which will be placed on the Arctic seabed (visit www.savethearctic.org to add your own name). It's part of a campaign to preserve the high Arctic as a 'global sanctuary' and ban offshore oil drilling and industrial fishing in the whole Arctic region. It's also made me think about all the things I do that are adding to global warming. From now on, I'll try to be much more careful with my energy use, for example. We must do everything we can to protect the beautiful, fragile Arctic.

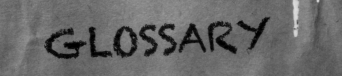

GLOSSARY

acclimatise Become used to a different climate or environment.

antibiotics Medicines that weaken or destroy bacteria.

axis An imaginary line about which an object, such as the Earth, rotates.

barricade An obstacle.

breathable fabric Fabric that admits air to the skin and allows sweat to evaporate.

buoyancy The ability to float in water.

carbon dioxide A colourless, odourless gas produced by burning carbon-containing materials, such as wood and vegetable matter.

cold snap A sudden, usually brief spell of very cold temperatures.

compensation Money awarded to someone to make up for loss, injury or suffering.

crevasse A deep, open crack in an ice sheet.

dehydration The loss of a large amount of water from the body.

electrically charged atom An atom that has lost or gained one or more electrons. Such atoms are also called ions.

fossil fuels Fuels, such as coal or gas, formed in the distant past from the remains of living organisms.

frostbite Injury to the body's tissues by exposure to extreme cold.

frostnip A mild form of frostbite, only affecting the skin.

global warming The gradual increase in the overall temperature of the Earth's atmosphere, due in part to human activities.

Gore-Tex® A breathable, waterproof fabric, used in outdoor and sports clothing.

hypothermia The condition of having a dangerously low body temperature.

ice crystals Particles of ice that are made up of highly symmetrical shapes.

ice floe A sheet of floating ice.

ice screw A threaded tube used to anchor something into the ice.

ice shelf A floating sheet of ice permanently attached to a landmass.

infrastructure The buildings, roads and power supplies of a settlement.

insulation Layers of material placed over the body to prevent loss of heat.

kayak A type of canoe made of a light frame with a watertight covering and a small opening at the top to sit in.

magnetic field The area around a magnet within which a force of magnetism acts. The Earth acts like a giant magnet and has its own magnetic field.

mirage An optical illusion caused by atmospheric conditions.

mollusc A family of soft-bodied organisms that includes snails, slugs, mussels and octopuses.

negative drift Movement of ice floes against the direction of travel.

North Magnetic Pole The point on the Earth's northern hemisphere where the planet's magnetic field points vertically downwards.

North Star A star, also called Polaris, that is located within one degree of the north celestial pole (an imaginary point in the sky directly above the Earth's axis of rotation) and is therefore useful for navigation.

open water lead Channel of water between ice floes.

pack ice An expanse of ice floes, driven together into a nearly continuous mass.

permafrost A thick, sub-surface layer of soil that remains frozen throughout the year.

polynia A large area of open water surrounded by sea ice.

precipitation Rain, snow, sleet or hail.

rationing Limiting the amount of something, such as food, allowed to each person, to ensure supplies last out.

snow bridge A drift of snow covering a crevasse.

solar wind A continuous stream of electrically charged atoms from the sun.

tissue Any of the different types of material of which humans, animals and plants are made.

INDEX & FURTHER INFORMATION

Books

The Frigid Arctic Ocean (Our Earth's Oceans) by Doreen Gonzales (Enslow Elementary, 2013)

How To Survive in the Arctic and Antarctic (Tough Guides) by Louise A Spilsbury (PowerKids Press, 2012)

Climate Change in the Arctic by Stuart Baker (Benchmark Books, 2009)

People of the North (Exploring the Canadian Arctic) by Heather Kissock and Audrey Huntley (Weigl Publishers, 2009)

Websites

http://www.bbc.co.uk/nature/places/Arctic
http://www.ehow.com/list_6306085_list-survival-tips-arctic.html
http://www.maxadventure.co.uk/NorthPole